PROBLEM PAGE

# ME AND MY FRIENDS

...DERSON

# W
# FRANKLIN WATTS
## LONDON · SYDNEY

# Problem Page
## Me and my friends

Relationships with friends are a very important part of our lives, but they are not always easy. The letters and emails in this book are from young people who are experiencing all kinds of problems. Some have chosen to confide in friends, while others have written to an advice column. A few have only told their diaries…

### Dear reader

The postal addresses used in this book have all been changed to fictitious places. The email addresses have also been censored. All the photographs are posed by models.

# He won't leave us alone

BB2A 7F

12 March

Steve Thomas Advice column
Geared-up magazine
Orley OPJ 6PF

**Dear Steve**

There's a boy in our class, Carl, who won't stop hanging around with us. He's really annoying and no one likes him. He always tries to be funny but he isn't, and he follows us around because he thinks we're all mates. He's even started coming skateboarding with us.

How can we get rid of him?

Tom and James
(aged 12)

## Carl's diary

12th March

School was a bit better today. Afterwards, I went skateboarding with Tom and James. Mum bought me all the gear last week. Now I've got the gear I think I fit in more, though Tom and James are best mates and I'll always be on the outside. It's Tom's birthday next week. Mum's going to give me a pocket-money advance so I can get him something good.

# What makes a good friend?

My friends stand up for me if I get picked on. It's best to have a lot of friends because then you can go out in a group and no one feels left out.

Gemma, aged 13

To be a good friend you have to be nice and kind and helpful. My best friend is to me. I've known her for five years. I think it's better to have one best friend than loads because if you've got loads, you always end up arguing.

Amy, aged 11

My best friends are my best friends because we don't have to pretend about anything with each other. We fall out sometimes but that's normal, isn't it?

Anthony, aged 11

## Top Tips
### Making friends

⭐ Clubs and activities are a great way to meet people without coming across as 'annoying'.

⭐ 'Buying' friends with gifts doesn't work.

⭐ Ask questions. If people feel you are interested in them, they are likely to be interested in you!

⭐ Don't be tempted to show off or make up things about yourself.

⭐ If you see someone who looks a bit lost and alone why not ask him or her to join in with your friends? It may not make much difference to you, but it might make someone else really happy.

⭐ Be open and honest, and don't forget to smile and be yourself!

## Your Views

What do you think Steve will tell Tom and James to do?

Should Carl stick with them or try to make different friends?

Is it best to have just a few friends, or lots?

# She sends nasty text messages

I've been watching U, picking yr spotty face.

U think U R so cool, but U don't have a clue.

Jon says U R thick.

Time to DIET, Mica!!!

## Mica's diary

**21 July**

Janine is sending me nasty text messages. I've had four today. I'm sure it's her, even though I don't recognise the number. She must be using someone else's phone.

I think she's doing it because I didn't let her borrow my new mobile. Now I feel like she's spying on me all the time, saying mean things about me and calling me fat or spotty. I tried talking to her today but she just looked at me like I was from another planet.

The messages are getting nastier. I want them to stop.

# The Facts

## A kind of bullying

✳ Some people use text messages as an easy way to get at someone. Sending nasty text messages or emails is a common form of bullying.

✳ Bullying means any type of persistent spiteful behaviour. It might include name-calling, spreading nasty rumours, or making threats.

✳ It is an offence to send bullying messages by phone or by email. Most 'electronic' bullies can be identified by their number, caller ID or email address, though this is not always possible.

✳ Phone companies should be told about persistent bullying as they can change your mobile number or even shut down a bully's account.

# Top Tips

## Don't let them get away with it

⭐ If you know the bully, you could send a message warning them that it is an offence to use a mobile phone in this way. However, do not be tempted to send them any threatening messages of your own.

⭐ If the bullying doesn't stop, tell a responsible adult and report the bully to the phone company or the police.

⭐ Save the nasty messages or emails as evidence.

⭐ Change your mobile number, or even get a new phone. It's not fair to have to do this, but it will stop the nasty messages.

⭐ Be careful about who you give your number to in the future. Some people decide to use their phones for emergencies only.

# Your Views

Mica is very upset about the messages she has received. Is she over-reacting?

Why do you think this kind of bullying is common?

# I don't want to change schools

56 Carillon St
Summerstown
SS44 5TU

26 July

23 Willow Street
Summerstown
SS22 8PM

**Dear Ruth**

I hope you're having a great holiday. I'm okay, but I'm really going to miss you when I start at my new school. All the girls there play volleyball at lunchtime, which I hate, and I don't think they do much drama, which is the only thing I'm any good at.

I'm worried that I won't make any friends, but in a funny sort of way I don't want to, either. You've always been my best friend. I just wish you were coming too.

I hope to see you soon.

Love Simone x

# The Facts
## Moving on

❋ Most children have to change schools at some point. Often this is a move to a more senior school, but sometimes it is because the family moves to a different area.

❋ A new school doesn't mean never seeing old friends; it means making new ones.

❋ Many schools have a variety of clubs and sports that are designed to help you make friends. Some schools even run a mentoring scheme to help new students settle in.

❋ Everyone is different. Making new friends often means being open to new ideas and interests. Friends aren't always the people who are most like ourselves.

# Top Tips
## Making it in a new school

⭐ Try to visit the school before you start there properly. (Your current school may be able to arrange this for you.) Finding out where to go and what to do on the first day will make you feel more comfortable.

⭐ Join an after-school club or try a new sport. You may feel shy at first, but group activities do help to break the ice and they also give you the opportunity to check out a variety of possible friends.

⭐ It can be off-putting if you talk too much about the fun you used to have with your old friends. No one wants to have to compete for your friendship.

# Your Views

Why is Simone reluctant to make new friends? How would you feel if you were her? What would you do?

# What if she fancies me?

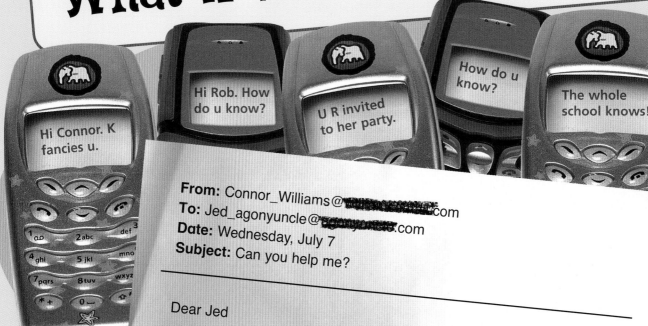

Hi Connor. K fancies u.

Hi Rob. How do u know?

U R invited to her party.

How do u know?

The whole school knows!

**From:** Connor_Williams@⬛⬛⬛⬛.com
**To:** Jed_agonyuncle@⬛⬛⬛⬛.com
**Date:** Wednesday, July 7
**Subject:** Can you help me?

Dear Jed

My mate Rob says that this girl Kate fancies me. He says I should ask her out, but it's not that simple. I really like her, we sometimes play football together, but I hate the way everyone goes on about us all the time. If I ask her out and she says no, then they'll all laugh at me. If she says yes then I might feel even more stupid. I don't know what to do.

Connor
(aged 12)

**From:** Jed_agonyuncle@~~████████~~.com
**To:** Connor_Williams@~~████~~
**Date:** Wednesday, July 7
**Subject:** Re: Can you help me?

Dear Connor

It is very hard to decide how you feel about someone when everyone is telling you what you should do. You obviously like Kate, but if you are not sure how she feels then it might be an idea to get to know her better so that you can find out for yourself, without relying on gossip from friends.

Don't feel pressured into asking her out. If you don't feel ready to have a girlfriend, it doesn't mean that you can't spend time with her. Perhaps you can do fun things together in a group. Maybe that's what she would like, too. Just do whatever feels right for you.

Yours, Jed
Agony uncle

# Are boyfriends and girlfriends worth having?

My friends all think it's cool to have a boyfriend.
Anna, aged 11

I don't want a girlfriend. I like hanging out in a group. It means I don't get left out of anything.
Mark, aged 12

My mates made stupid comments when I went out with Gemma. She didn't care, but it really bothered me.
Cal, aged 12

'Going out' can mean lots of different things. It might mean going on a date somewhere, or it might just mean holding hands on the way home from school.
Sarah, aged 10

# Your Views

Do you think Connor should tell Kate how he feels? Does it matter what their friends think?

# They hate me because I'm black

**From:** Laurence@e~~verybod~~mail.com
**To:** Jed_agonyuncle@~~agonyuncle~~.com
**Date:** Tuesday, October 15
**Subject:** Message for agony uncle

Dear Jed

I'm being bullied at school. A group in the year above me have been spreading rumours about my dad, and sometimes they kick me or push me in the playground. At first I thought they were being mean to all the younger kids, but then someone wrote 'blackie' on my locker and there has been some new graffiti in the toilets saying stuff like 'blackie go home'. I know they mean me. One of the girls called me an 'alien' the other day. They hate me because I'm black.

If I tell my dad he'll go ballistic. He'll call the school racist and things will probably just get worse. I don't want trouble. I want to be left alone.

Laurence
(aged 10)

**From:** Jed_agonyuncle@~~agonyuncle~~.com
**To:** Laurence@~~everyone~~mail.com
**Date:** Tuesday, October 15
**Subject:** Re: Message for agony uncle

Dear Laurence

Bullying someone because of their race, colour, nationality or culture is often called racial abuse. It is a particularly nasty and dangerous form of bullying, because the bullies are not only attacking you as an individual, they are also attacking your family and others in the community like you.

You must tell a teacher or an older student you can trust. Keep an incident diary too, recording the people involved, the date and the time. Racial bullying is an offence, and your school will probably want to deal with the bullies as effectively as possible. This might mean some fuss at first, but in the long run it should mean that you are no longer a victim. It might also send a signal to others that racial bullying will not be tolerated.

Finally, don't give up on your dad. If you explain your fears, he might agree to deal with the school without getting angry.

Jed, Agony Uncle

# What do you think of racial bullying?

> Bullies who pick on people because of their skin colour are too stupid to think of anything else to do.
>
> Toby, aged 11

> You can be a bully without being racist, and you can be a racist without being a bully. But a racist bully is two bad things in one.
>
> Tanysha, aged 13

> We are refugees from Afghanistan. My parents thought we'd be safe here. They didn't expect me to be bullied because of where I'm from.
>
> Saira, aged 11

## Your Views

Laurence doesn't want a fuss, but his dad prefers angry confrontation. Do you think there are more effective ways of dealing with racial bullying in school?

15

# They think it's funny

254 Wilberforce Street
Peninghill
NSW 4621

Dear Harry

Thanks for the birthday card. I had a great day. Mum bought me a basketball hoop so me, Jon and Adam were playing with that. Jon and Adam are annoying me though. They think it's funny to go around slapping people on the cheek all the time. I feel like hitting them back when they do it to me. I know they're not trying to start a fight or anything – they just do it for a laugh but sometimes it really hurts.

I don't want to get them into trouble because they're my mates, but I want them to stop it. Any ideas?

How is your new sister? Mum says we will come and visit her soon.

Nicholas

# Top Tips

## What is acceptable?

⭐ If your friends are doing this sort of thing to you, don't do it back. Tell them that you don't like it.

⭐ If the problem persists, tell an adult you trust. Otherwise your friends will continue to do it, and they may end up really hurting someone.

⭐ A pat on the back or a nudge in the ribs might be acceptable among friends, but always ask yourself if you'd mind if someone did it to you.

⭐ Slapping or hitting is never friendly, or funny. Don't do it or tolerate it.

# Is it okay to get physical?

Rugby is very physical and aggressive. What's the difference between organised sport and a bit of wrestling in the playground?

Alex, aged 12

I used to go to a school where the boys did neck holds on each other. One boy ended up in hospital. After that we got detention if we even touched each other.

Luke, aged 11

I fight with my sister all the time. I don't know why, except that she is totally annoying.

Aisling, aged 9

Me and my friend sometimes push each other around a bit. We don't mean anything by it.

Raul, aged 11

# Your Views

Should Nicholas complain about his friends? Do you think there is a difference between rough play and aggressive behaviour?

17

# Her dad doesn't like me

**From:** mina@~~████████~~.com
**To:** Jules@~~████████~~.com
**Date:** Thursday, February 9
**Subject:** Saturday

Hi Julie

Thanks for inviting me over on Saturday. I'd really like to come but you know what my dad's like – he wants to know exactly what we'll be doing and I know he'll make a fuss if I tell him we're going to the cinema. He doesn't want me to sleep over either. Could you just come over for a couple of hours in the afternoon?

See you then.

Mina

Suzanne Jones, Agony Aunt
Girls' Together Magazine
Treefield TR15 9PG

Dear Suzanne

I have a good friend called Mina and we get on really well at school, but I don't think her dad likes me. He never lets Mina come to my house, and he seems to think I'm a bad influence on her or something. Maybe it's because she's a Muslim and I'm not.

The trouble is, she won't argue with him and always goes along with whatever he says. If he told her she couldn't be friends with me any more, I think she'd do it. Why can't she stand up for me sometimes? That's what friends do isn't it?

Regards

Julie (aged 13)

Suzanne Jones
Girls' Together Magazine
Treefield

15 July

44 Rosemont Road
Treefield TR21 4AR

Dear Julie

It sounds as though you are a loyal friend to Mina, but it might help to try to put yourself in her shoes sometimes. After all, she has chosen you as a friend, too. Her dad may be worried about her for all sorts of reasons which may be to do with her religion, or may not. Perhaps Mina's dad just needs to get to know you a bit better. If he has any specific worries such as staying out late then you might be able to reassure him.

Both Mina and her dad need to know they can trust you. It may seem a bit unfair, but hopefully your friendship with Mina will make it all worthwhile.

Best wishes

Suzanne, Agony Aunt

# Do differences matter in your friendships?

Best friends don't have to come from the same background, but they should respect each other's differences.

Devon, aged 12

I choose my friends, but I can't choose their parents!

Ali, aged 11

As long as we have a laugh together and enjoy each other's company, I don't care about anything else.

Lizzie, aged 14

# Your Views

Do you think Mina should do what her dad wants? Should she stand up for Julie?

# I haven't told her

Hi Kim! Sat next to Chris on bus. He's gorgeous!

Hi Layla. What did he say?

Not much but I think he wants to go out with me!

13 November

## Kim's diary

Layla thinks Chris fancies her. I know I should tell her that Chris and I have been going out, but I can't do it. She'll be really upset and she'll probably be mad at me for not telling her sooner. I don't know why I haven't. I don't know what to do now. Layla is a good friend and I don't want to hurt her, but Chris is my boyfriend and there's no way she's going to get her hands on him! Maybe I'll write her a letter...

# Will your love life change your friendships?

Me and my friend both fancied the same boy. It brought us closer because we spent so much time talking about him.

Phillippa, aged 10

I think my boyfriend is my best friend. I don't know what I'd do if he stopped going out with me.

Karen, aged 12

When my mate Tom had a girlfriend he stopped playing football after school. He was really boring for a while. Then his girlfriend dumped him. Now he's back on the team.

Liam, aged 12

I've got a girlfriend but my friends are okay about it. We still do loads of boys-only stuff.

George, aged 13

## Top Tips
### Changing relationships

★ Be honest with your friends. Try to explain how you feel. Your friends are more likely to be understanding if you don't keep them in the dark.

★ Your friends may feel a bit excluded when you start to go out with someone. Let them know that you still want to spend time with them. Otherwise they may think that you no longer value their friendship.

★ Try not to see relationships as a competition. There are no winners or losers; good friendships are about supporting each other and wanting each other to be happy.

## Your Views

What would you do if you were Kim? Do you think she should stop going out with Chris?

# Internet friends

**From:** seananderson@~~mymail.com~~

**To:** agonyuncle@~~magazinehouse~~.com

**Date:** Tuesday, September 1

**Subject:** Meeting up with my chatroom friend

---

Dear Charlie

I've been emailing Ben for about three months. We met in a chatroom and have a lot in common – he likes mountain-biking as well. I email him every evening – my mum thinks I'm using the computer for homework. I can't wait to get home from school and get online. When I was having a hard time with my mum a few weeks ago, Ben really helped me.

Last week, Ben suggested that we meet up. I'd really like to meet him, but my mum always has to know where I am so I'd have to tell her about Ben. What should I do? I don't want to let Ben down because he's sort of my best friend. But I think mum would want to come along, and that would be really embarrassing.

Sean
(aged 11)

**From:** agonyuncle@~~fudgelandhouse~~.com
**To:** seananderson@~~myrealllll~~
**Date:** Tuesday, September 1
**Subject:** Re: meeting up with my chatroom friend
**Attachment:** Factsheet - Internet safety

---

Dear Sean

Please be very careful. It's very easy to pretend you are someone else on the Internet. Mostly people just exaggerate things about themselves, but sometimes they are complete liars. 'Ben' could actually be a grown man who has an unhealthy interest in young boys. You can't be sure.

Please tell your mum what is happening. If you decide to meet Ben, suggest that your mum does go along. If Ben objects, he's not a real friend – real friends make sure their mates are comfortable and happy.

Charlie, Agony Uncle
PS I've attached a factsheet with some tips for safe surfing.

## Charlie's factsheet - Internet safety

Chatrooms and messaging can be great fun, but remember, you never really know who you are talking to online. To make sure you are safe:

- Never use your real name in chatrooms – pick a special online nickname.
- If you arrange to meet up with someone you've only spoken to online, be careful; only meet them in public places and take an adult.
- Never respond to nasty or rude messages, and don't send them either!
- Be careful with any email attachments or links that people send you. They might contain nasty images, or computer viruses that could ruin your PC.
- Don't let it take over your life! Keep up your other interests and try to use the Internet with friends and family, not just on your own.

# Your Views

How would you respond to Ben if you were in Sean's situation?

Would you tell your parents?

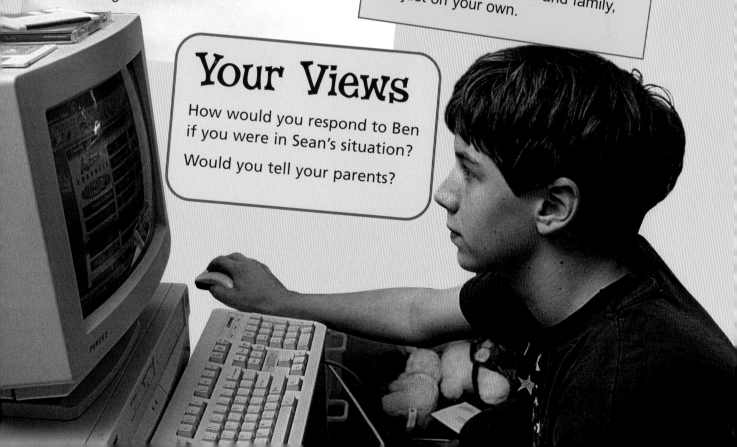

# She bosses me about

**From:** caitlin@~~████~~.com
**To:** anaomiquinn@~~████~~.com
**Date:** Friday, April 10
**Subject:** Shopping

---

Hi Naomi

I'm glad the week's over! Science was BORING today. I hope you're coming out with us tomorrow – not with Patrick again. Don't know why you hang out with him – have you seen his scabby trainers? Be at the bus stop at 11am and we'll meet the others there.

Caitlin

## Naomi's diary

### Friday, April 10

Caitlin wants me to go shopping with her tomorrow but I'm not sure. She'll expect me to get something expensive and trendy. She always wears designer stuff. Patrick says she and her friends all look the same, but then he doesn't care if he wears embarrassing trainers. I don't want Caitlin to talk about me the way she talks about him.

# Do you just want to fit in?

People who don't follow the crowd are more independent.

Dominic, aged 11

Everyone wants to be seen wearing the right label, but designer clothes are too expensive. I hate being ripped off.

Rob, aged 12

Good friends don't put pressure on each other. They don't mind if you wear the 'wrong' trainers!

Ciara, aged 10

I think it's OK to want nice clothes, but it's not OK for people to tease you if you don't have them.

Ayesha, aged 9

## Top Tips
### Fitting in

⭐ Most of us want to fit in and be part of a group. However, if this means doing something you don't want to do, it's unlikely that you are ever going to feel really comfortable in that group. It might be time to find some different friends.

⭐ Sometimes people can be quite mean if we don't do what they want. Practise saying no in front of the mirror or make up an excuse that might help you, but if someone is being really mean you should tell someone you can trust.

⭐ Wearing the 'right' clothes is all about fitting in. That's fine, but you can also have fun creating your own style.

## Your Views

How easy is it to say no to someone like Caitlin?

What would you do if you were Naomi?

# I'm afraid to go out

R22 8TF

30 March

Steve Thomas Advice column
Geared-up magazine
Orley OPJ 6PF

Dear Steve

There's a gang of boys on our estate who hang around by the garages. I have to walk past them to get to school and it's like they're waiting for me. Sometimes they just take my money, but if this boy Nate is there he throws stuff at me – bottles, sticks, bits of brick. He says I'm a moving target. He also says that if I tell anyone he'll come and find me, and then I'll be sorry.

All this week I've pretended to be sick so that I don't have to go to school. I hate being such a wimp but I'm too afraid to go out. Do you know what I should do?

Christian
(aged 11)

## Christian's diary

I'm really frightened of Nate. He knows where I live. I can't tell Mum though because she knows some of the other mums and Nate would find out. She probably wouldn't believe me anyway.

I wish I could just disappear.

Steve Thomas Advice column
Geared-up magazine
Orley OPJ 6PF
5 April

If you are being bullied, try some of the following tips:

- Stick in a group – bullies usually pick on kids who are alone.

- Keep an incident diary.

- Tell someone you can trust, like a friend or a teacher or your parents. They will usually be able to help, and sharing your fears will make you feel stronger.

- If possible, try to laugh at a bully's behaviour or tell them to get lost (you could practise in the mirror first). Remember that they want you to feel scared.

- If you see someone else being bullied, tell an adult.

19 Carlton Rise
Rugfield R22 8TF

Dear Christian

You are not a wimp. Remember that Nate and his friends are bullies, and bullies are often cowards who use force or verbal abuse to make themselves feel strong. What these bullies are doing is illegal, and they may well be doing it to other kids as well. Anyone in your situation would feel afraid.

However, there are people who can help you, and there are things you can do to help yourself. If you don't want to tell your mum, could you tell a teacher or someone in the police? These people are trained to deal with bullies, and your name wouldn't have to be involved. Also, think about whether you can take a different route to school, or ask a friend if they could walk with you.

I have enclosed a factsheet with some tips about bullying.

Steve, Agony Uncle

# Your Views

Do you think Christian should tell his mum? Would it help if he talked separately to the boys his mum knows?

# Glossary

**Bullying** any kind of persistent, spiteful behaviour. Bullying includes verbal abuse, threats of any kind, hitting and pushing, spreading nasty rumours, name-calling or deliberately ignoring someone.

**Chatrooms** Internet sites where you can meet and exchange messages with other people online. There is no face to face contact.

**Electronic bullying** spreading nasty rumours or sending threatening or spiteful messages by email or by phone texting.

**Incident diary** a diary of bullying activity which can be used as evidence. Usually includes time, place, people involved and what happened.

**Mentoring** a scheme often used in schools in which an older pupil acts as a guide for a younger pupil and helps them with any difficulties they may be experiencing.

**Peer pressure** when you feel you must be the same as your friends and peers because you want to be part of a group and not be left out. This pressure may affect the clothes you wear, the way you behave and the things you say you like and dislike.

**Racial abuse** bullying someone because of their race, colour, nationality or culture.

**Racist** someone who hates or fears certain people purely because of their race, colour, nationality or culture.

**Refugee** someone who has fled their country because of war, famine, poverty or prejudice.

**Respect** a vital element of friendship and relationships in general. Respect means appreciating someone else for who they are, accepting their point of view and not invading their personal space.

**Trust** another important aspect of friendship. It means that you feel you can depend on someone. Trust means not revealing a secret, keeping a promise, not doubting that what someone says is true and being loyal. Remember, however, you should not always trust what someone says in an Internet chatroom.

# Websites

**UK**

**www.school-resources.co.uk**
Go to 'Student Common Room' and click on 'Problem Page' for advice on friendships and settling into a new school.

**www.bullying.co.uk**
Straightforward help and advice for victims of bullying.
Email: help@bullying.co.uk

**www.kidscape.org.uk**
Site of a charity helping to prevent bullying and child abuse. Useful Frequently Asked Questions section.

**www.childline.org.uk**
Download factsheets on bullying and friends. Good advice page on Internet safety. Childline runs a free and confidential 24-hour helpline: 0800 1111

**www.thinkuknow.co.uk**
Clear, friendly tips on how to stay safe while having fun online.

**www.youngminds.org.uk/education**
Look under 'Info for Young People' for advice about making friends and coping with peer pressure.

**AUSTRALIA**

**www.cyh.com.au**
Child and Youth Health site, divided into separate sections for kids and young people. Try 'Your School' for help with friendships, peer pressure, moving schools and bullying. Try 'Your Feelings' for more help with friendship issues.

**www.kidshelp.com.au**
Information and links on bullying.

**www.racismnoway.com.au**
'Games Room' page with quizzes, comics and games designed to challenge racism at school.

# Index

aggressive behaviour 16, 17

bullying 9, 14, 15, 26, 27

chatrooms 22, 23
clubs 11

emails 9, 22, 23

fitting in 25
friends 7, 11, 16, 17, 18, 19, 24, 25
    best friends 7, 19, 21
    boyfriends 13, 20, 21
    girlfriends 13, 21
    making friends 7, 10, 11

Internet 22, 23

mentoring 11
mobile phones 8, 9

parents 14, 15, 18, 19, 27
peer pressure 13, 24, 25

racism 14, 15

teachers 15, 27
text messages 8, 9

First published in 2005 by Franklin Watts
96 Leonard Street, London EC2A 4XD

Franklin Watts Australia
45-51 Huntley Street,
Alexandria, NSW 2015

© Franklin Watts 2005

Series editor: Sarah Peutrill
Art director: Jonathan Hair
Design: Rita Storey
Picture researcher: Diana Morris
Advisor: Wendy Anthony, Health education consultant

ISBN 0 7496 6044 9

Printed in Hong Kong/China